D0531834

Experiments With Electricity

SUSAN H. GRAY

Children's Press®
An Imprint of Scholastic Inc.
New York Toronto London Auckland Sydney
Mexico City New Delhi Hong Kong
Danbury, Connecticut

Content Consultant
Suzanne E. Willis, PhD
Professor and Assistant Chair, Department of Physics
Northern Illinois University
DeKalb, Illinois

Library of Congress Cataloging-in-Publication Data

Gray, Susan Heinrichs.
  Experiments with electricity/Susan H. Gray.
      p. cm.—(A true book)
  Includes bibliographical references and index.
  ISBN-13: 978-0-531-26344-0 (lib. bdg.)   ISBN-13: 978-0-531-26644-1 (pbk.)
  ISBN-10: 0-531-26344-4 (lib. bdg.)   ISBN-10: 0-531-26644-3 (pbk.)
  1. Electricity—Experiments—Juvenile literature. I. Title.
  QC527.2.G73 2012
  537.078—dc22   2011009398

All rights reserved. Published in 2012 by Children's Press, an imprint of Scholastic Inc.
Printed in China 62
SCHOLASTIC, CHILDREN'S PRESS, A TRUE BOOK, and associated logos are trademarks and/or registered trademarks of Scholastic Inc.

1 2 3 4 5 6 7 8 9 10 R 21 20 19 18 17 16 15 14 13 12

Find the Truth!

Everything you are about to read is true *except* for one of the sentences on this page.

Which one is **TRUE**?

T or F A balanced atom has no electrical charge.

T or F A scientist's hypothesis is always correct.

Find the answers in this book.

Ben Franklin

Contents

THE **BIG** TRUTH!

Tesla's Big Ideas

Nikola Tesla

4

You can do the experiments with electricity in this True Book.

4 Current Electricity

5 Electricity Gets Even Better!

About 75 percent of all copper used in the United States is used to carry electricity.

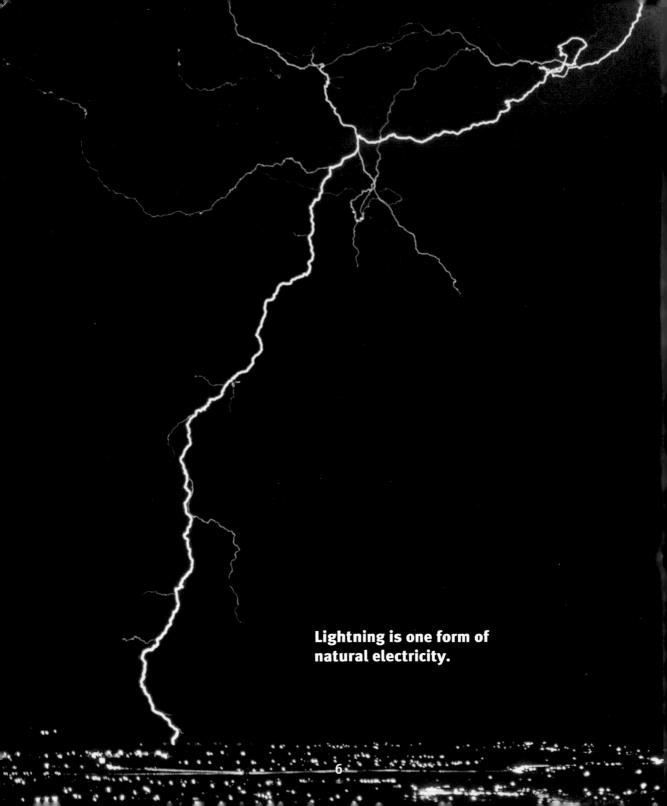

Lightning is one form of natural electricity.

The Scientific Method

Thousands of years ago people saw electricity at work. They did not do experiments, but they did make **observations**. For example, they saw lightning and noticed that it started fires and split trees in two. Today, scientists study electricity by doing experiments. Scientists almost always follow a system called the scientific method. It is a step-by-step process for finding answers.

The energy of one lightning bolt could power a home for a month!

How It Works

This is how the scientific method works. First, a scientist pulls together all the observations about something. Next, he or she thinks up a question that the observations don't explain.

Then the scientist forms a **hypothesis**. This is what the scientist believes is the correct answer to the question. It must be a statement that can be tested. Next, he or she plans out an experiment to test it.

Scientists perform research to learn about other scientists' observations.

Scientists use special symbols to make diagrams of electrical circuits.

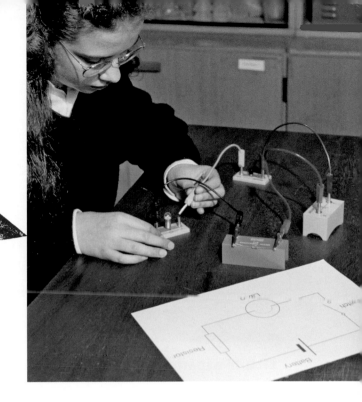

Experiments enable scientists to find answers to their questions.

During the experiment, the scientist writes down everything that happens. Finally, the scientist looks at how the experiment turned out and draws a **conclusion**.

Sometimes, the conclusion is that the hypothesis is correct. Other times, it turns out that the hypothesis was not correct. Then it's time to come up with a new hypothesis and design another experiment.

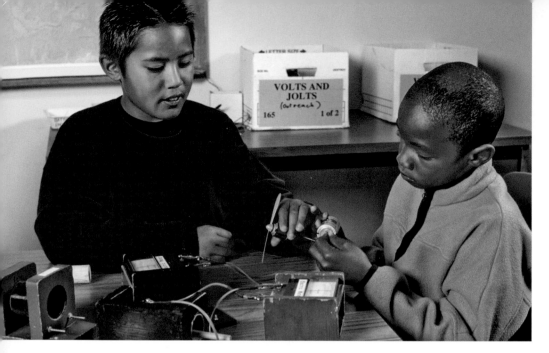

Simple experiments can help you learn how electricity works.

Things to Remember

When scientists do experiments, there are several things they must remember. The first thing is to keep an open mind. Suppose a scientist creates a hypothesis and designs an experiment to test it. What if the experiment shows that the hypothesis was incorrect? The scientist can run the experiment again to see if it turns out the same way.

But what if the experiment does turn out the same way? Then the scientist must be willing to learn from the experience. He or she must accept that the hypothesis is wrong and think about what needs to be changed.

Good scientists also measure everything carefully during an experiment. They **record** their steps and measurements in a notebook. This way, they can always look back and see exactly how they did the experiment.

Everything in a lab notebook is written in ink to keep data readable in case of accidents, such as spills.

Scientists keep careful records of their experiments.

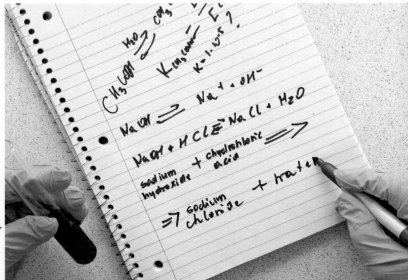

We use electrical
devices such as hair
dryers every day.

12

CHAPTER 2

What Is Electricity?

To understand electricity, we have to learn about **atoms**. Everything in the universe is made up of incredibly small atoms. Atoms are made up of smaller particles called **electrons**, **protons**, and **neutrons**.

Protons and neutrons are packed together at the center, or **nucleus**, of the atom. Electrons spin at top speed around the nucleus. Each electron has a negative charge. Each proton has a positive charge. Neutrons have no charge.

Millions of electrons flow through the electrical cord to power this hair dryer.

Balanced and Unbalanced Atoms

In general, an atom has the same number of electrons and protons. That means it has the same number of negative and positive charges. In this state, the atom is balanced and stable. An atom, however, does not always stay this way. Remember, the electrons are spinning around the nucleus. Sometimes one of these zooming electrons gets knocked off.

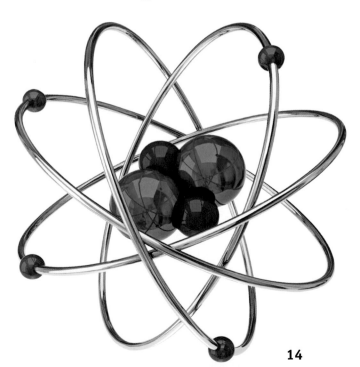

Scientists use colored balls and rings to create models of atoms.

Sometimes you can get a small shock of electricity by touching a doorknob.

You can see sparks caused by jumping electrons if you are in a dark room.

If an electron gets knocked off, the numbers of protons and electrons in the atom are no longer equal. The atom has one more proton than it has electrons. Then it has an overall positive charge. The electron that gets knocked off can stick to another atom. That atom will then have one more electron than it has protons. It will have an overall negative charge.

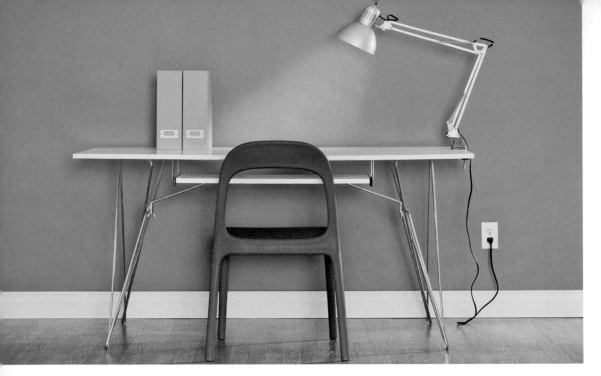

We use wires and outlets to control the path of electricity in our homes.

Electric Current

Sometimes, electrons can be forced to move from one atom to the next and the next. When electrons flow like this, they set up a current of electricity. This is what happens inside an electrical cord from a wall outlet. "Loose" electrons move from one metal atom in the wire to the next. They follow a path from the outlet, down the wire, and to an appliance.

Conductors

Some materials are made of atoms that give up their electrons readily. It is easy to knock electrons off. This is the case with copper, aluminum, steel, and other metals. These are exactly the materials used inside electrical wires. Their loose electrons easily flow from one atom to the next, creating a current. Because these materials conduct a current so easily, they are called conductors.

Most homes have copper wiring. ➡

Electricians must be careful when working with exposed electrical wires so that they don't get electrocuted.

Overhead power lines often have glass or porcelain insulators on the poles.

Huge amounts of electricity travel to our homes and businesses through overhead power lines.

Insulators

Other materials are made of atoms that hold tightly to their electrons. These are materials such as rubber, plastic, and glass. It is very difficult to get an electric current to run through them. That is why materials such as these are used as the outer covering for electrical cords and wires. They are called insulators.

Static Electricity

In current electricity, electrons flow in one direction following a definite path. In static electricity, electrons behave a little differently. Loose ones do not follow a definite path. Instead, they build up on the surface of some material. Have you ever rubbed your feet on a carpet and then touched a metal doorknob? The shock you feel is the result of static electricity.

Static electricity can cause a balloon to stick to your sweater.

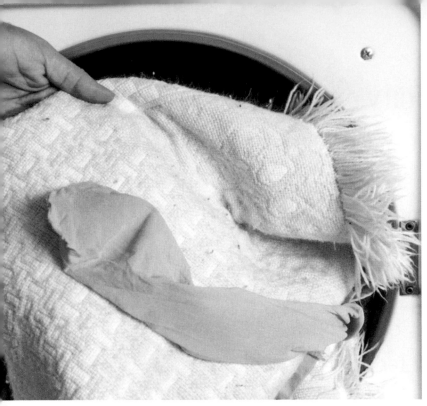

Fabric softener uses special chemicals to prevent static electricity in clothes dryers.

Static electricity can cause clothes to stick together in the dryer.

Opposites Attract

There is one more thing to know about atoms. They tend to remain balanced and stable, with no overall charge. When an atom loses an electron, it "looks for" an available electron to fill the space. Likewise, a free electron looks for an atom that needs it to become balanced.

An atom with a positive charge needs an electron. And a free electron, with its negative charge, needs a positive atom. In short, opposite charges attract each other. At the same time, particles with the same charges will move away from—or **repel**—each other.

In the next few chapters, we will show how current and static electricity work. We will first perform demonstrations. Then we will try some experiments based on those demonstrations.

Glass can become electrically charged if it is rubbed against certain materials.

You might experience static electricity during winter when you take a fabric hat off!

Static Electricity

Before we do any experiments, we will show static electricity at work in a demonstration.

Demonstration: Sticky Balloons

Materials:
- ▶ **A balloon**
- ▶ **About 10 inches (25 centimeters) of string**
- ▶ **A wool sweater or scarf**

Procedure:

1. Blow up the balloon and tie it off.

2. Tie the end of the string to the balloon.

3. Rub the balloon rapidly back and forth on the sweater or scarf.

4. Dangle the balloon near a wall.

Observe: Because of static electricity, the balloon swings toward the wall.

What happened? The cloth fibers of the sweater or scarf easily gave up their electrons to the balloon. As the balloon nears the wall, electrons and protons in the wall rearrange themselves. The protons move closer to the balloon because the balloon is negative and attracts protons. The balloon is covered with electrons. It moves toward the wall's protons.

Experiment #1: Two Balloons

Observe: A balloon rubbed against a scarf creates static electricity.

Research question: What happens if two balloons are rubbed against a scarf or sweater?

True Book hypothesis: The balloons will move away from each other.

Materials:

- **2 balloons**
- **2 pieces of string, each about 10 inches (25 cm) long**
- **wool scarf or sweater**

Procedure:

1. Blow up both balloons and tie them off.

2. Tie a piece of string to each balloon.

3. Rub both balloons against the scarf or sweater.

4. Dangle the balloons near each other.

Record your results: How do the balloons behave?

Conclusion: Both balloons became negatively charged when rubbed against a scarf or sweater. As a result, the balloons repel each other. They move apart. Does this match your observations? Was the True Book hypothesis correct?

Step 3

Experiment #2: Moist Air

Research question: Will the balloon keep its negative charge in moist air?

True Book hypothesis: The balloon will not move toward the wall in moist air.

Materials:
- **steamy bathroom, possibly after running a hot shower**
- **balloon**
- **string**
- **wool sweater or scarf**

Many of these materials were used in the demonstration (p. 23)

Procedure: Repeat steps 1 through 4 of the demonstration (p. 23), this time in a steamy bathroom.

Record your results: How does the balloon behave?

Conclusion: The moisture in the air pulled the electrical charge away from the balloon. The balloon was left with no charge. It could not stick to the wall. Does this match your observations?

A Mysterious Substance

Amber is dried, hardened tree sap. It is golden in color. In ancient Greece, a **philosopher** named Thales noticed something. When he polished a lump of amber, it did strange things. It attracted feathers, dust, straw, and other lightweight objects to itself. When he wiped the amber off, these objects jumped back on again. Thales did not understand what was going on. He did not know about static electricity.

Tesla's Big Ideas

As a child in the 1860s, Nikola Tesla longed to visit New York and see Niagara Falls. Tesla liked science and dreamed of harnessing the falls' power.

Eventually, he moved to New York and got the chance to help design a power plant at Niagara Falls. The plant used an alternating current (AC) motor invented by Tesla. Today, power plants using the ideas of Tesla and other inventors provide electricity all around the world.

Tesla grew up in Europe and moved to New York as a young man.

When Tesla first moved to New York, he worked for the inventor Thomas Edison.

Tesla eventually had his own laboratory.

Current Electricity

Current electricity comes through wall sockets and from batteries. For our demonstration and experiments, we will use batteries. First, let's do a demonstration.

Demonstration: Electric Loop

Be Safe: You should have an adult help you when you experiment with electricity.

Materials:

> **small utility knife or wire stripper**
> **2, 10-inch (25 cm) pieces of 30-gauge insulated copper wire**
> **flashlight bulb with threads**
> **masking tape**
> **1 D battery**

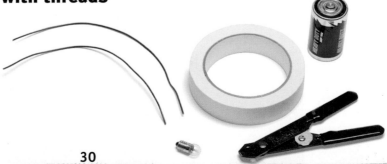

Procedure:

1. Ask an adult to trim about 1 inch (2.5 cm) of the insulation from all the wire ends.

2. Wrap the end of one wire around the threaded part of the bulb.

3. Tape the wire's free end to the negative (flat) end of the battery.

4. Tape one end of the other wire to the positive end of the battery.

5. Lightly tap the positive wire on the bottom of the flashlight bulb.

Step 3

31

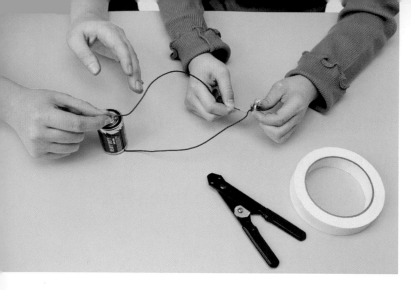

Step 5
Tapping the end of the wire to the bottom of the bulb completes a circuit.

Observe: The bulb should light up.

What happened? The bulb lights up because an electrical current is flowing in a loop, or **circuit**. The electrons flow from the battery and down the wire. Then they flow to the bulb, down the other wire, and back to the battery. The electrons flow as long as you hold the wire to the bottom of the bulb.

Experiment #1: Is It Metal?

Observe: Mylar looks like shiny metal.

Research question: Is Mylar metal? If it is, it should conduct electricity.

True Book hypothesis: Mylar is metal.

Materials:
- 2, 10-inch (25 cm) strips of Mylar
- flashlight bulb with threads
- masking tape
- 1 D battery

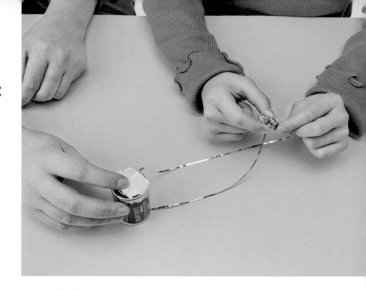

Can Mylar conduct electricity?

Procedure: Repeat steps 2 through 5 of the demonstration (p. 31), using Mylar strips instead of wire.

Record your results: Does the flashlight bulb light up?

Conclusion: Mylar is an insulator, not a metal. Like rubber or glass, it can't easily carry an electrical current. Because of this, there was no circuit and the bulb didn't light up. Does this match your observations? Was the True Book hypothesis correct?

Experiment #2: Is Bigger Better?

Research question: Does a thicker wire conduct more electricity?

True Book hypothesis: A thicker wire carries more electricity.

Materials:
- ▶ **the circuit created in the demonstration (pp. 30–31)**
- ▶ **2, 10-inch (25 cm) pieces of 18-gauge insulated copper wire (thicker than the wire used before)**
- ▶ **flashlight bulb with threads**
- ▶ **masking tape**
- ▶ **1 D battery**
- ▶ **small utility knife or wire stripper**

Timeline of Electricity

About 600 B.C.E.
Greek thinker Thales notices static electricity on amber.

1752 C.E.
Ben Franklin proves that lightning is a form of electricity.

1800
Alessandro Volta of Italy invents the battery.

Procedure: Repeat steps 1 through 5 of the demonstration (p. 31), using the thick copper wire.

Record your results: Compare what happens to the bulb in each circuit. Do they look the same?

Conclusion: The thicker wire can carry a stronger electrical current. The stronger current makes the bulb's light brighter. Does this conclusion match your observations? Was the True Book hypothesis correct?

1895
Nikola Tesla designs the Niagara Falls power plant.

1897
Joseph John Thomson discovers the electron.

1954
First nuclear power plant begins providing electricity in Russia.

CHAPTER 5

Electricity Gets Even Better!

In 1820, a teacher named Hans Oersted discovered that he could create a magnet by using electricity. In this demonstration, we'll use his discovery.

Demonstration: Building an Electromagnet

Be Safe: You should have an adult help you when you experiment with electricity.

Materials:

- **large nail**
- **3 or 4 paper clips**
- **about 4 feet (1.2 meters) of magnetic wire (from an electronics store or hobby shop)**
- **fine sandpaper**
- **electrical tape**
- **1 D battery**

Gather these materials.

Procedure:

1. Touch the nail head to the paper clips and lift it up. What happens? **Step 7**

2. Gently sand off the insulation from both ends of the wire.

3. Wrap the wire around the nail many times. It's ok to overlap the wire when you are wrapping.

4. Leave about 6 inches (15 cm) of the wire straight at both ends.

5. Tape one end of the wire to the battery's negative end.

6. Tape the other wire end to the battery's positive end.

7. Touch the nail to the paper clips and lift up.

8. Be Safe: Remove one end of the wire from the battery. Leaving both ends can cause things to get hot.

Observe: The nail picks up the paper clips easily.

What happened? The nail contains iron. The iron becomes magnetized from the electric current encircling it.

Experiment #1: Smaller

Research question: What would happen if you used a smaller nail?

True Book hypothesis: The nail is still a magnet.

Materials:
- **small nail**
- **paper clips**
- **magnet wire**
- **fine sandpaper**
- **electrical tape**
- **1 D battery**

Many of these materials were used in the demonstration (p. 36).

Procedure:

1. Wrap the wire around a small nail. Leave about 6 inches (15 cm) of the wire straight at both ends.
2. Repeat steps 5 through 8 of the demonstration (p. 37).

Record your results: Does the nail pick up paper clips? How many?

Conclusion: The nail should have picked up fewer paper clips than the larger nail did in the demonstration. Because it is smaller, it carries a weaker magnetic field. Does this match your observations? Was the True Book hypothesis correct?

Roller coasters use electromagnets to run cars along their tracks.

Experiment #2: Aluminum Nail

Research question: Can aluminum be used to create an electromagnet?

True Book hypothesis: Aluminum cannot be used to create an electromagnet.

Materials:
- **large piece of aluminum foil**
- **paper clips**
- **magnet wire**
- **electrical tape**
- **1 D battery**

Many of these materials were used in the demonstration (p. 36).

Procedure:

1. Roll the aluminum foil to the size of the iron nail.

2. Repeat steps 3 through 8 of the demonstration (p. 37).

Record your results:

Did the aluminum nail pick up any paper clips?

Conclusion: The aluminum couldn't pick up paper clips. Aluminum contains no iron. A material needs iron to become magnetic. Does this match your observations?

Ben's Bells

Ben Franklin helped shape U.S. government, but he also liked to experiment with electricity. At one time, he placed a tall iron rod atop his chimney. He ran a wire from it down into his house and connected it to little bells. Ben noticed that "when clouds passed with electricity in them" sometimes the bells rang. Maybe Franklin's "lightning bells" were the first storm warning system.

Amazing Electricity

Electricity is an incredible force. It can be stored in batteries. It can run through power lines. Electricity can be drawn from lightning storms. It can be generated by the power of a waterfall. Electricity lights the largest of modern cities. And it shows up on ancient chunks of amber. Electricity is truly amazing! ★

It takes a lot of electricity to power a big city such as New York.

First electric car: An electric carriage developed by Robert Anderson of Scotland in the 1830s

How often planes are struck by lightning: On average, once a year

Number of times lightning strikes: Worldwide, about 100 times every second, or more than 8.6 million times each day

Percentage of people who survive lightning strikes: 90 percent, but often with serious injuries

Best natural conductor: Pure silver, followed by copper

Animal that shocks: Electric eels, which can emit electrical surges 5 times stronger than a household current

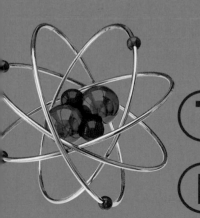

Did you find the truth?

(T) A balanced atom has no electrical charge.

(F) A scientist's hypothesis is always correct.

Resources

Books

Adamczyk, Peter, and Paul-Francis Law. *Electricity and Magnetism*. Tulsa, OK: EDC Publishing/Usborne Books, 2008.

Aldrich, Lisa. *Nikola Tesla and the Taming of Electricity*. Farmington Hills, MI: Kidhaven Press, 2005.

Editors of Time for Kids. *Thomas Edison: A Brilliant Inventor*. New York: HarperCollins, 2005.

Norman, Penny. *Electricity*. El Sobrante, CA: Norman & Globus, 2006.

Stillinger, Doug. *Battery Science: Make Widgets That Work and Gadgets That Go*. Palo Alto, CA: Klutz, 2003.

Venezia, Mike. *Benjamin Franklin: Electrified the World With New Ideas*. New York: Children's Press, 2010.

Venezia, Mike. *Thomas Edison: Inventor With a Lot of Bright Ideas*. New York: Children's Press, 2009.

Organizations and Web Sites

Institute of Physics

www.physics.org/explore.asp
Do a search for electricity at this site to find pages with
amazing facts and fun experiments.

National Geographic: Lightning

http://environment.nationalgeographic.com/environment
/natural-disasters/lightning-profile.html
Read about lightning, then scroll down to an interactive page
and make lightning strike.

Tesla Memorial Society of New York

www.teslasociety.com
Learn more about Nikola Tesla's life and inventions.

Places to Visit

American Museum of Radio and Electricity

1312 Bay Street
Bellingham, WA 98225
(360) 738-3886
http://amre.us//
In addition to seeing the exhibits, visitors can take mini-classes in electronics.

Thomas Edison National Historical Park

211 Main Street
West Orange, NJ 07052-5612
 (973) 736-0550
www.nps.gov/edis/index.htm
See some of Edison's inventions and try some hands-on activities.

Important Words

atoms (AT-uhmz)—the tiniest parts of an element that have all the properties of that element

circuit (SIR-kuht)—the complete, looped path of an electric current

conclusion (kuhn-KLOO-zhun)—final decision

electrons (i-LEK-trahnz)—tiny, negatively charged particles that move around the nucleus of an atom

hypothesis (hy-PAH-thuh-siss)—a prediction that can be tested about how a scientific experiment or investigation will turn out

neutrons (NOO-trahnz)—one of the extremely small parts that form the nucleus of an atom; neutrons have no electrical charge

nucleus (NOO-klee-uhs)—the central part of an atom that is made up of neutrons and protons

observations (ob-zur-VAY-shuhnz)—things that are learned while watching, hearing, or otherwise sensing events

philosopher (fih-LOSS-uh-fer)—someone who loves knowledge and thinks deeply

protons (PROH-tahnz)—positively charged particles inside a nucleus

record (rih-KORD)—to write down

repel (rih-PEHL)—to push away something

Index

Page numbers in **bold** indicate illustrations

About the Author

Susan H. Gray has a master's degree in zoology and has done research on plankton and on fish development. She has also written more than 120 books for children. Susan especially likes to write on topics that engage children in science. She and her husband, Michael, live in Cabot, Arkansas.